31-Day Devotional For Teenagers:

Standing Strong

Volume 1

A Journey to Unshakable Faith in a Broken World

'KIITAN OYEDUN

31-DAY DEVOTIONAL FOR TEENAGERS

Standing Strong

Published by Cornerstone Publishing

A Division of Cornerstone Creativity Group LLC
Info@thecornerstonepublishers.com
www.thecornerstonepublishers.com

Author's Contact

To book the author to speak at your next event or to order bulk copies of this book, please, use the information below:

authors@crescitebooks.com

For Crescite Books updates and notification about upcoming books, reach out to:

info@crescitebooks.com

Printed in the United States of America.

FOREWORD

Over the past eighteen years, I have been privileged to share the path of life with a number of young people as they navigate identity, purpose, faith, life decisions to name a few. The questions they ask as they tussle with these life issues have not changed in those eighteen years. The themes remain consistent over the years. I watch their zest for knowledge, hunger for truth, genuine confusion sorting through information thrown at them and the climax of relief when they pray through their struggles and arrive at Christ-centered solutions to life problems.

This devotional is a great guide for such a time as this. It is Bang & Olufsen in a world inundated with so much noise both in the circular sphere and in spiritual discussions. It is a simple, well-guided and honest compass for young people seeking to delve into scriptures as the source of answers to their contemplations.

This resource hits different, I must say. It is set in a warm tone that draws you in and meets you at whatever level you are on your faith journey as a young person. You will find it to be a safe place to ask your questions as you study, receive answers as you spend time meditating on the words, scriptures, and declarations for each day, and in turn build necessary spiritual habits that will help you become a well formed young person rooted and grounded in God's word. The result will be a young person ready for the long haul.

Finally, the scope of this devotional covers every fundamental life moment that you may encounter as a young person. You realize that you are not alone and need not go it alone.

It is my prayer that as you devour this devotional, you will feel enlightened, encouraged, strengthened, and guided through your faith journey, on a day-to-day basis. May you increase in faith as you discover and wholly embrace your identity in Christ in Jesus name.

'Yemi Philip

HOD The Royal Seeds,
RCCG Rhema Chapel Teenage Church

CONTENTS

PREFACE

Welcome to a journey that could change your life.

Let's be real for a moment. Being a teenager in today's world is not easy. You're navigating a culture that celebrates everything God calls you away from. You're facing pressure from every side: friends, social media, school, and even your own desires. Sometimes it feels like you're fighting a battle that no one else understands.

But here's the truth: You're not alone, and you're not powerless.

God has called you to stand strong in a world that's falling apart. He's equipped you with everything you need to live victoriously, not as a victim of culture, but as a conqueror through Christ. This devotional isn't about religious rules or empty religion. It's about real faith that works in real life. It's about discovering who you are in Christ and learning to stand firm when everything around you is shaking.

Over the next 31 days, you'll dive deep into God's Word, declare truth over your life, and take practical steps that will transform the way you live. Each day is designed to be short enough to fit into your busy schedule but powerful enough to impact your entire day. You'll find a memory verse to hide in your heart, a devotional thought to challenge your thinking, declarations to speak over your life, an action step to put faith into practice, and a prayer to guide your conversation with God.

This isn't just another devotional you read and forget. This is a battle plan. A roadmap. A toolkit for standing strong against the darkness of this world.

Are you ready? Let's do this. Your breakthrough starts today.

DAY 1

You Are Chosen, Not Forgotten

Memory Verse

But you are not like that, for you are a chosen people. You are royal priests, a holy nation, God's very own possession. As a result, you can show others the goodness of God, for he called you out of the darkness into his wonderful light — *1 Peter 2:9, NLT.*

Bible Reading: *1 Peter 2:9-12*

Devotional:

Have you ever felt invisible? Like no one really sees you or understands what you're going through? Maybe you scroll through social media and wonder if you'll ever matter like everyone else seems to. Here's the truth that changes everything: God handpicked you before the world began. You're not an accident, a mistake, or just another face in the crowd. You are chosen royalty with a divine purpose. The same God who created galaxies knows your name and called you His own. When the world tries to define you by your failures, your appearance, or your popularity, remember that your identity is locked in heaven. You belong to the King of Kings, and that makes you royalty. Today, walk like you know who you are.

Prayer:

Father, I pray that You would help me to see myself the way You see me. Remind me daily that I am chosen, loved, and purposed for Your glory. When the world tries to tell me I'm not enough, speak Your truth over my life. Help me to walk confidently in my identity as Your child in Jesus name.

Declarations:

- I speak life over my identity: I am chosen by God, not by the world's standards.

- I declare that I am royalty in God's kingdom, set apart for His purpose.

- I speak boldly: My worth is not determined by likes, followers, or opinions, but by the One who created me.

Action Step:

Write down three specific reasons you believe God chose you. Consider your unique gifts, personality, and story. Post a note somewhere you'll see it daily that says, "I am chosen."

Journal Space:

DAY 2

Guard Your Heart Like Your Life Depends On It

Memory Verse

Keep vigilant watch over your heart; that's where life starts – Proverbs 4:23, MSG.

Bible Reading: *Proverbs 4:20-27*

Devotional:

Your heart is like a garden. Whatever you plant there will grow, whether good or bad. Every song you listen to, every video you watch, every conversation you have is planting seeds. Some seeds produce beautiful flowers of faith, hope, and love. Others grow into weeds of doubt, fear, and compromise. The scary part? You might not notice the weeds until they've taken over. That toxic friendship? That show everyone watches, but makes you feel empty inside? That music that glorifies everything God calls you away from? These are not harmless. They're shaping who you're becoming. God isn't being a fun-killer when He asks you to guard your heart. He's protecting your future. What enters your heart today becomes your character tomorrow. Be ruthless about what you allow in.

3

Prayer:

Lord, help me to be vigilant in guarding my heart. Give me discernment to recognize what is harmful and courage to remove it from my life. Protect my heart from the things that would lead me away from You. Fill me with Your truth and purity. In Jesus name.

Declarations:

- I speak protection over my heart: I will guard it fiercely against anything that dishonours God.

- I declare that I have the wisdom to recognize what is harmful and the courage to remove it.

- I speak this truth: My heart is God's dwelling place, and I will keep it holy

Action Step:

Do a heart audit today. Check your social media, your playlists, and your screen time. Delete or unfollow one thing that you know pulls you away from God. Then, replace it with something that builds your faith.

Journal Space:

DAY 3
Resist The Trap And Watch The Enemy Run

Memory Verse

So then, surrender to God. Stand up to the devil and resist him, and he will turn and run away from you – James 4:7, TPT.

Bible Reading: *James 4:1-7*

Devotional:

Temptation isn't a sign that you're weak or that you're failing God. Jesus Himself was tempted, and He never sinned. The difference between falling and standing is what you do in that moment of pressure. The enemy sets traps everywhere: that text from someone you know you shouldn't be talking to, that party where you know things will go down that contradict your values, that shortcut that requires you to lie. Here's the game-changer: You don't have to negotiate with temptation. You don't have to entertain it or see how close you can get without falling. James says when you resist the devil, he runs away. Not walks. Not strolls. He flees. But resistance starts with submission to God. Get close to Him first, and the strength to say no becomes supernatural. You're not fighting alone.

Prayer:

Father, I pray that You would give me supernatural strength to resist every temptation that comes my way. Help me to surrender fully to You so that I can stand firm against the enemy's schemes. When I'm weak, be my strength in Jesus name.

Declarations:

- I speak authority over every temptation: In Jesus' name, I have the power to resist.

- I declare that I will not negotiate with sin or flirt with compromise.

- I speak victory: When I resist the enemy, he must flee because greater is He who is in me.

Action Step:

Write down your biggest temptation right now. Pray specifically about it. Then, create a practical plan: When tempted today, pause, pray one sentence ("Jesus, help me"), and walk away or change the situation immediately.

Journal Space:

....

....

....

....

DAY 4
Be The Light When Darkness Feels Normal

Memory Verse

You are the light of the world—like a city on a hilltop that cannot be hidden – Matthew 5:14, NLT.

Bible Reading: *Matthew 5:14-16*

Devotional:

Look around your school, your team, your friend group. Darkness is normal now. Cruelty is funny. Purity is mocked. Integrity is old-fashioned. It's easy to feel like your little light doesn't matter when the darkness seems so overwhelming. But here's what Jesus said: You ARE the light. Not you might be, or you could be, or try to be. You ARE. And light always, always defeats darkness. Even a small flame in a pitch-black room changes everything. You don't have to be the loudest person or the most popular to make a difference. You just have to let your light shine. That might look like sitting with the lonely kid at lunch. Refusing to laugh at the cruel joke. Choosing kindness when everyone else chooses mockery. Speaking up when everyone else stays silent. Your light disrupts the darkness, and that makes the enemy nervous.

Prayer:

Lord, help me to shine brightly for You in every situation. Give me the courage to be a light in the darkness and to show Your love to those who need it most. Don't let me hide my light or compromise to fit in, in Jesus name.

Declarations:

- I speak light into every dark space I enter: I carry the presence of Jesus with me.

- I declare that my kindness, my words, and my actions will point people to God.

- I speak boldly: I will not hide my light to make others comfortable with their darkness.

Action Step:

Today, intentionally shine your light by doing one act of kindness for someone who is overlooked, bullied, or alone. Don't do it for recognition. Do it because you carry the light of Christ.

Journal Space:

DAY 5
No Compromise, No Regrets

Memory Verse

But Daniel resolved not to defile himself with the royal food and wine, and he asked the chief official for permission not to defile himself this way – Daniel 1:8, NIV.

Bible Reading: *Daniel 1:8-21*

Devotional:

Daniel was a teenager when he was taken captive to Babylon. He could have easily justified compromising. "Everyone else is doing it." "It's just food, it doesn't really matter." "I need to fit in to survive here." But Daniel drew a line. He resolved in his heart before the pressure came. That's the key. You can't wait until you're in the moment to decide what you stand for. Peer pressure is designed to prompt a reaction, not encourage thoughtful consideration. By the time your friends are pressuring you to compromise, it's too late to figure out your values. Daniel made his decision beforehand, and God honoured it. He didn't just survive in Babylon; he thrived. When you refuse to compromise, God shows up and shows off. It might be lonely at first, but you'll never regret standing firm. You will regret caving.

Prayer:

Father, I pray that You would give me the courage to stand firm in my convictions, even when everyone around me is compromising. Help me to resolve in my heart now what I will and will not do, so that I'm prepared when pressure comes. Honour my commitment to You in Jesus name.

Declarations:

- I speak resolution over my life: I will decide now what I stand for so I won't fall when pressure comes.

- I declare that I will not compromise my values for acceptance, popularity, or comfort.

- I speak this truth: God honours those who honour Him, and I will trust Him with the outcome.

Action Step:

Identify one area where you face the most pressure to compromise (relationships, partying, honesty, purity, etc.). Write down your boundary and why it matters. Share it with one trusted person who will hold you accountable.

Journal Space:

DAY 6
Renew Your Mind, Change Your Life

Memory Verse

Stop imitating the ideals and opinions of the culture around you, but be inwardly transformed by the Holy Spirit through a total reformation of how you think. This will empower you to discern God's will as you live a beautiful life, satisfying and perfect in his eyes – Romans 12:2, TPT.

Bible Reading: *Romans 12:1-8*

Devotional:

Your mind is a battlefield. Every day, the world bombards you with messages: "You're not enough." "This is what success looks like." "Everyone's doing it." "You deserve to do whatever makes you happy." These messages are patterns, and if you're not careful, you'll conform to them without even realizing it. But God offers transformation, not through trying harder, but through renewing your mind. That means replacing the world's lies with God's truth. You can't binge on negativity all week and expect to think positively. You can't fill your mind with junk and expect to make wise decisions. Transformation happens when you intentionally fill your mind with Scripture, worship, and truth. It's not a one-time thing; it's a daily choice. Renew your mind, and watch your life change.

Prayer:

Lord, help me to renew my mind daily with Your truth. Transform the way I think so that I can see clearly what Your will is for my life. Break the patterns of this world that try to shape me and mould me into Your image instead, in Jesus name.

Declarations:

- I speak transformation over my mind: I will not conform to the world's patterns.

- I declare that God's Word will be my source of truth, not social media, not culture, not popular opinion.

- I speak renewal: Every day, I will replace one lie with God's truth.

Action Step:

Today, replace one negative or worldly thought with Scripture. Write the verse on your phone's lock screen or on a sticky note. Every time that thought creeps in, speak the verse out loud.

Journal Space:

DAY 7

True Strength Comes From Dependence

Memory Verse

For I can do everything through Christ, who gives me strength – Philippians 4:13, NLT.

Bible Reading: *Philippians 4:10-20*

Devotional:

We live in a culture that worships self-sufficiency. "You don't need anyone." "Be your own hero." "Believe in yourself." It sounds empowering, but it's exhausting. The truth is, you weren't designed to do life alone. Real strength isn't about flexing your independence; it's about depending on Jesus. Paul wrote this verse from prison. He wasn't living his best life. He wasn't on a mountaintop. He was in chains, yet he had strength because his source wasn't himself. When you try to be strong on your own, you'll burn out. But when you plug into God's strength, you'll discover power you never knew you had. Dependence isn't weakness. It's wisdom. Stop trying to white-knuckle your way through life. Let God be your strength.

Prayer:

Father, I pray that You would be my strength in every situation. Help me to stop relying on myself and to depend fully on You. When I am weak, remind me that Your power is made perfect in my weakness. I need You every moment of every day in Jesus name.

Declarations:

- I speak this truth: My strength does not come from myself, but from Christ who lives in me.

- I declare that I will stop trying to do life on my own and will depend on God daily.

- I speak boldly: In my weakness, God's power is made perfect, and I will lean on Him.

Action Step:

Face one challenge today (a test, a difficult conversation, a temptation) by praying first instead of relying on your own strength. Before you act, pause and say, "Jesus, I need You for this."

Journal Space:

DAY 8
Your Circle Shapes Your Character

Memory Verse

Don't let yourselves be poisoned by this anti-resurrection loose talk. Bad company ruins good habits – 1 Corinthians 15:33, MSG.

Bible Reading: *1 Corinthians 15:29-34*

Devotional:

Show me your friends, and I'll show you your future. That might sound harsh, but it's true. You become like the people you spend the most time with. If your friends are constantly pulling you toward compromise, negativity, and sin, you will drift. It's not a matter of if, but when. You might think you're strong enough to resist their influence, but God's Word says otherwise. Bad company corrupts good character. It's not about being judgmental or thinking you're better than anyone. It's about being honest: Are your friendships drawing you closer to God or further away? Are they building your faith or eroding it? This doesn't mean you can't have friends who don't share your faith. But your closest circle, the people who influence you most, need to be people who sharpen you, not dull you. Choose wisely.

Prayer:

Lord, help me to choose my friendships wisely. Surround me with people who will encourage my faith and challenge me to grow closer to You. Give me the courage to distance myself from relationships that pull me away from Your will in Jesus name.

Declarations:

- I speak wisdom over my friendships: I will choose friends who draw me closer to God.

- I declare that I will not compromise my values to keep friendships that pull me down.

- I speak protection: God will surround me with people who sharpen my faith and encourage my walk.

Action Step:

Evaluate your friendships honestly. Make a list of your closest friends. Next to each name, write whether they pull you closer to God or further away. Pray about any changes you need to make, and intentionally invest more in the friendships that build you up.

Journal Space:

....

....

....

DAY 9
Sometimes The Right Move Is To Run

Memory Verse

Run from anything that stimulates youthful lusts. Instead, pursue righteous living, faithfulness, love, and peace. Enjoy the companionship of those who call on the Lord with pure hearts – 2 Timothy 2:22, NLT.

Bible Reading: *2 Timothy 2:14-26*

Devotional:

There's a time to stand and fight, and there's a time to run. When it comes to certain temptations, especially those tied to youthful desires, God doesn't say "Be strong and resist." He says, "Flee." Run. Get out. Don't stay and see if you can handle it. Joseph fled from Potiphar's wife. He didn't try to reason with her or prove his strength. He ran, and God honoured him. Some situations are not meant to be wrestled with. That relationship that constantly pulls you toward sexual compromise? Flee. That environment where everyone's getting drunk or high? Flee. That conversation that always leads to gossip or tearing others down? Flee. Running isn't cowardice. It's wisdom. It's saying, "I know my limits, and I'm not playing with fire." Flee evil and chase righteousness with the same intensity.

Prayer:

Father, I pray that You would give me wisdom to know when to stand and when to run. Help me to be humble enough to flee from situations that would compromise my purity and my relationship with You. Give me the courage to run toward righteousness instead, in Jesus name.

Declarations:

- I speak wisdom: I will know the difference between when to stand and when to run.

- I declare that I will not be ashamed to flee from temptation because my purity matters more than my pride.

- I speak commitment: I will pursue righteousness with the same passion the world pursues sin.

Action Step:

Identify one situation or environment where you need to flee, not fight. Make a practical exit plan. If it's a relationship, a place, or a habit, decide today how you'll remove yourself when temptation comes.

Journal Space:

....

....

....

....

DAY 10
Your Words Have Power, Use Them Wisely

Memory Verse

Your words are so powerful that they will kill or give life, and the talkative person will reap the consequences – Proverbs 18:21, TPT.

Bible Reading: *Proverbs 18:19-24*

Devotional:

Words are not just sounds. They're seeds. They carry life or death. Think about the last time someone said something cruel to you. Those words probably still echo in your mind. Now think about a time someone spoke life over you. Those words probably still fuel you. You have that same power. Your words can tear someone down or build them up. They can spread hope or despair. And here's the hard truth: You will eat the fruit of your words. If you constantly speak negativity, gossip, and cruelty, that's what your life will become. But if you choose to speak life, encouragement, and truth, you'll reap a harvest of blessing. Before you post, text, or speak, ask yourself: Is this giving life or death? Your words matter more than you think.

Prayer:

Lord, help me to use my words wisely. Let everything that comes out of my mouth bring life, encouragement, and hope to those around me. Convict me when my words are harmful, and help me to apologize and make it right in Jesus name.

Declarations:

- I speak life: My words will build up, not tear down.

- I declare that I will guard my tongue and speak with wisdom, kindness, and truth.

- I speak this commitment: I will encourage at least one person today with my words.

Action Step:

Send a text, write a note, or speak face-to-face to someone and genuinely encourage them. Share something you appreciate about them or how they've positively impacted you. Watch how your words bring life.

Journal Space:

DAY 11

Hide God's Word
In Your Heart

Memory Verse

I have hidden your word in my heart that I might not sin against you – Psalm 119:11, NIV.

Bible Reading: *Psalm 119:9-16*

Devotional:

Memorizing Scripture might feel old-school or unnecessary in a world where you can Google anything. But there's a difference between knowing where to find truth and having truth embedded in your heart. When temptation hits, you won't have time to pull out your phone and search for a verse. But if God's Word is hidden in your heart, the Holy Spirit will bring it to your mind exactly when you need it. Jesus defeated Satan in the wilderness by quoting Scripture. He didn't say, "Hold on, let me check my Bible app." He had God's Word ready. That's the power of memorization. It's your weapon in battle. It's your comfort in pain. It's your guide in confusion. Start small. Pick one verse this week. Write it. Say it. Repeat it until it's locked in your heart.

Prayer:

Father, I pray that Your Word would take deep root in my heart. Help me to memorize Scripture and to recall it when I need it most. Let Your Word be a lamp to my feet and a light to my path in Jesus name.

Declarations:

- I speak commitment: I will hide God's Word in my heart so I'm ready for every battle.

- I declare that Scripture will be my first defense against temptation and my source of truth in confusion.

- I speak this truth: God's Word is alive, active, and powerful in my life.

Action Step:

Memorize today's memory verse. Write it on a notecard and carry it with you. Say it out loud at least five times throughout the day until you can recite it without looking.

Journal Space:

DAY 12

Your Identity Is In Christ, Not In Likes

Memory Verse

My ego is no longer central. It is no longer important that I appear righteous before you or have your good opinion, and I am no longer driven to impress God. Christ lives in me. The life you see me living is not 'mine,' but it is lived by faith in the Son of God, who loved me and gave himself for me – Galatians 2:20, MSG.

Bible Reading: *Galatians 2:15-21*

Devotional:

How many times a day do you check your phone for validation? Likes. Comments. Views. Follows. We've become addicted to affirmation from people who don't even know us. And when the validation doesn't come, we feel worthless. Here's the problem: You're building your identity on sand. People's opinions shift. Trends change. What's popular today is forgotten tomorrow. But your identity in Christ is unshakable. You are loved, chosen, forgiven, and empowered, not because of what you do, but because of who He is. When Christ lives in you, your worth is no longer up for debate. It's settled. You don't need the approval of people who are just as insecure as you are. You have the approval of the God who created the universe. Let that sink in and change how you see yourself.

Prayer:

Lord, help me to find my identity in You alone, not in the approval of others. Remind me daily that I am loved, chosen, and valued by You. Break my addiction to validation from social media and people in Jesus name.

Declarations:

- I speak life over my identity: I am not defined by likes, followers, or popularity.
- I declare that my worth is found in Christ alone, and nothing can change that.
- I speak this boldly: I am loved, chosen, and accepted by God, and that is enough.

Action Step:

Write a declaration of your identity in Christ. Start with "I am..." and list at least five truths from Scripture (loved, forgiven, chosen, a child of God, etc.). Read it every morning this week.

Journal Space:

....

....

....

....

DAY 13
Fight With Faith, Not Fear

Memory Verse

Fight the good fight for the true faith. Hold tightly to the eternal life to which God has called you, which you have declared so well before many witnesses – 1 Timothy 6:12, NLT.

Bible Reading: *1 Timothy 6:11-16*

Devotional:

Life is a fight. You're in a battle, whether you realize it or not. But the question is, what are you fighting with? Fear or faith? Fear says, "What if I fail? What if I'm rejected? What if I'm not strong enough?" Faith says, "God is with me. He's already won. I can do this." Fear paralyzes. Faith propels. The fight of faith isn't about mustering up your own strength or pretending you have it all together. It's about taking hold of the eternal life and the promises God has given you. When you're anxious, faith says, "God is in control." When you're tempted, faith says, "Greater is He who is in me." When you're discouraged, faith says, "God is working all things for my good." Stop fighting with fear. Fight with faith, and watch how the battle shifts.

Prayer:

Father, I pray that You would replace my fear with faith. Help me to trust You completely, even when I can't see the way forward. Strengthen my faith so that I can fight victoriously every day in Jesus name.

Declarations:

- I speak faith over fear: I will not let anxiety and doubt control my life.

- I declare that God is with me, and I will trust Him even when I can't see the outcome.

- I speak victory: I am fighting with faith, and God has already won the war.

Action Step:

Today, when fear or doubt creeps in, speak one promise of God out loud. Find a verse about God's faithfulness or His presence, and declare it over your situation.

Journal Space:

....

....

....

....

....

....

DAY 14

Keep Your Eyes And Heart Pure

Memory Verse

What bliss you experience when your heart is pure! For then your eyes will open to see more and more of God – Matthew 5:8, TPT.

Bible Reading: *Matthew 5:1-12*

Devotional:

Purity isn't popular. In fact, it's mocked. But Jesus said the pure in heart are blessed. Not weak. Not boring. Not missing out. Blessed. Purity isn't just about sex. It's about what you look at, what you listen to, what you entertain in your mind. It's about keeping your heart and eyes clean in a world that glorifies filth. This is hard. You can't avoid every temptation, but you can choose what you dwell on. You can choose to look away. To turn off the show. To swipe past the post. Purity is a fight, but it's worth it. God promises that those who pursue purity will see Him. Not in some distant heaven, but now. A pure heart creates space for God's presence. Don't trade that for a few minutes of pleasure that leaves you feeling empty.

Prayer:

Lord, help me to keep my heart and eyes pure. Give me the strength to turn away from anything that would compromise my purity and my relationship with You. Create in me a clean heart and renew a right spirit within me in Jesus name.

Declarations:

- I speak purity over my eyes and my heart: I will guard what I see and what I entertain in my mind.

- I declare that I will pursue holiness, not because I'm perfect, but because I love God.

- I speak this truth: Purity is not weakness; it's strength, and God will honour my pursuit of it.

Action Step:

Identify one media source (show, account, music, website) that compromises your purity. Delete it, unfollow it, or block it today. Replace it with something that builds your faith.

Journal Space:

DAY 15
Put On The Armour Of God Daily

Memory Verse

Put on all of God's armour so that you will be able to stand firm against all strategies of the devil – Ephesians 6:11, NLT.

Bible Reading: *Ephesians 6:10-20*

Devotional:

You wouldn't go into a physical battle without armour, so why do you try to face spiritual battles without it? Every day, you're in a war. The enemy wants to destroy your faith, your purity, your joy, and your purpose. But God has given you armour. The belt of truth. The breastplate of righteousness. The shoes of the gospel of peace. The shield of faith. The helmet of salvation. The sword of the Spirit. This isn't symbolic fluff. This is your daily protection. You put on the armour by praying, reading Scripture, choosing truth over lies, walking in righteousness, and standing firm in faith. Don't walk into your day unarmed. Take a few minutes every morning to intentionally put on the armour of God, and watch how the enemy's attacks lose their power.

Prayer:

Father, I pray that You would clothe me with Your full armour today. Cover me with Your truth, righteousness, peace, faith, salvation, and Your Word. Protect me from every attack of the enemy and help me to stand firm in battle in Jesus name.

Declarations:

- I speak protection over my life: I am clothed in the full armour of God.

- I declare that I will not face any battle unprotected; I will put on God's armour daily.

- I speak boldly: The enemy's schemes will not succeed because I stand firm in God's strength.

Action Step:

Pray through the armour of God today. As you name each piece, visualize putting it on and ask God to protect that area of your life.

Journal Space:

DAY 16
Courage Defeats Fear Every Time

Memory Verse

Haven't I commanded you? Strength! Courage! Don't be timid; don't get discouraged. God, your God, is with you every step you take – Joshua 1:9, MSG.

Bible Reading: *Joshua 1:1-9*

Devotional:

Fear is loud. It screams at you that you're not good enough, strong enough, or brave enough. It tells you to play it safe, stay quiet, and blend in. But God calls you to courage. Notice God didn't say, "Feel strong and courageous." He said, "Be strong and courageous." Courage isn't the absence of fear. It's moving forward in spite of it. It's speaking up when your voice shakes. It's standing alone when everyone else sits down. It's choosing what's right even when it costs you. God promises to be with you wherever you go. That means you're never facing anything alone. When fear whispers, "You can't," courage shouts, "God can, and He's with me." Today, choose courage over comfort, and watch what God does.

Prayer:

Lord, help me to be strong and courageous in every situation. When fear tries to paralyze me, remind me that You are with me every step I take. Fill me with Your courage so that I can stand firm for what is right in Jesus name.

Declarations:

- I speak courage over my life: I will not let fear dictate my decisions.

- I declare that God is with me everywhere I go, and that gives me the strength to be bold.

- I speak this truth: Fear is a liar, but God's presence is my courage.

Action Step:

Do one thing today that scares you but honours God. Share your faith with someone. Stand up for what's right. Say no to peer pressure. Choose courage, not comfort.

Journal Space:

....

....

....

....

....

DAY 17
Love In A Hateful World

Memory Verse

But I tell you, love your enemies and pray for those who persecute you, that you may be children of your Father in heaven. He causes his sun to rise on the evil and the good, and sends rain on the righteous and the unrighteous – Matthew 5:44-45, NIV.

Bible Reading: *Matthew 5:43-48*

Devotional:

Love is the most radical thing you can do in today's world. Not the fake love that agrees with everything. Not the easy love that only extends to people who are like you. The real, gritty, sacrificial love that Jesus showed. Love that serves when it's inconvenient. Love that forgives when it's hard. Love that chooses kindness even when it's not returned. This kind of love is countercultural because the world runs on hate, division, and revenge. But Jesus calls you to a higher standard. Walking in love doesn't mean being a doormat. It means reflecting the character of Christ even when it costs you. It means loving your enemies, praying for those who hurt you, and choosing compassion over cruelty. When you love like Jesus, you disrupt the darkness and point people to Him.

Prayer:

Father, I pray that You would fill me with Your extravagant love. Help me to love others the way You love me, even when it's difficult. Teach me to see people through Your eyes and to respond with grace and compassion in Jesus name.

Declarations:

- I speak love into every interaction: I will choose kindness, compassion, and grace.

- I declare that I will love like Jesus, even when it's hard and even when it's not returned.

- I speak this commitment: I will be known for my love, not my judgment.

Action Step:

Show love to someone who has hurt you or someone you typically avoid. It could be as simple as a kind word, a smile, or choosing not to retaliate. Let your love reflect Jesus.

Journal Space:

DAY 18

Fix Your Eyes On Jesus, Not The Distractions

Memory Verse

We look away from the natural realm and we fasten our gaze onto Jesus who birthed faith within us and who leads us forward into faith's perfection. His example is this: Because his heart was focused on the joy of knowing that you would be his, he endured the agony of the cross and conquered its humiliation, and now sits exalted at the right hand of the throne of God! – Hebrews 12:2, TPT.

Bible Reading: *Hebrews 12:1-13*

Devotional:

Distractions are everywhere. Your phone buzzes. Your feed refreshes. Your mind wanders. It's hard to focus on anything for more than a few seconds. But God calls you to fix your eyes on Jesus. Not glance. Not to check in occasionally. Fix. That means locking your focus and refusing to be pulled away. When you fix your eyes on Jesus, everything else fades into the background. The opinions of others lose their grip. The temptations lose their appeal. The fears lose their power. Jesus is the pioneer and perfecter of your faith. He's not just cheering you on from the sidelines. He's the one carving the path and finishing what He started in you. But you have to keep your eyes on Him. Stop letting distractions steal your focus. Limit your screen time. Turn off notifications. Spend time in His presence. Fix your eyes on Jesus, and your life will align.

Prayer:

Lord, help me to keep my eyes fixed on You alone. Remove every distraction that pulls my attention away from what truly matters. Teach me to prioritize time with You above everything else in Jesus name.

Declarations:

- I speak focus over my life: I will fix my eyes on Jesus, not on distractions.

- I declare that Jesus is my priority, and I will give Him my full attention.

- I speak commitment: I will limit distractions and spend intentional time with God daily.

Action Step:

Today, set aside 10 minutes of uninterrupted time with Jesus. No phone. No music. Just you and Him. Pray, read Scripture, or sit in silence and listen.

Journal Space:

DAY 19
Strength Through Humility

Memory Verse

Humble yourselves before the Lord, and he will lift you up in honour – James 4:10, NLT.

Bible Reading: *James 4:1-10*

Devotional:

Pride is sneaky. It doesn't always appear to be arrogance. Sometimes it looks like self-reliance. Sometimes it appears to be refusing to ask for help. Sometimes it looks like thinking you've got it all figured out. But pride will isolate you and set you up for a fall. Humility, on the other hand, is true strength. It's admitting when you're wrong. It's asking for help when you need it. It's recognizing that you don't have to prove anything to anyone. Jesus modelled humility perfectly. He, the King of Kings, washed His disciples' feet. He humbled Himself to the point of death on a cross. And because of that humility, God exalted Him. The same is true for you. When you humble yourself before God, He lifts you up. Stop trying to elevate yourself. Let God do it.

Prayer:

Father, I pray that You would teach me true humility. Help me to lay down my pride and to trust that You will lift me up in Your perfect timing. Give me a servant's heart like Jesus had in Jesus name.

Declarations:

- I speak humility over my life: I will admit when I'm wrong and ask for help when I need it.

- I declare that I don't have to prove my worth because God has already declared it.

- I speak this truth: Humility is strength, and God will honour it.

Action Step:

Do one humble act today without seeking credit. Serve someone. Help behind the scenes. Apologize if you need to. Let your humility reflect Jesus.

Journal Space:

....

....

....

....

....

....

DAY 20
Set Apart, Not Just Different

Memory Verse

None of this fazes us because Jesus loves us. I'm absolutely convinced that nothing—nothing living or dead, angelic or demonic, today or tomorrow, high or low, thinkable or unthinkable—absolutely nothing can get between us and God's love because of the way that Jesus our Master has embraced us – Romans 8:37, MSG.

Bible Reading: *Romans 8:31-39*

Devotional:

You're not called to blend in. You're called to be set apart. That doesn't mean you're better than anyone else. It means you belong to God, and your life should reflect that. Being set apart might look like choosing integrity when everyone else is cheating. Choosing purity when everyone else is hooking up. Choosing kindness when everyone else is cruel. You won't always fit in, and that's okay. You were never meant to. But here's the promise: You are more than a conqueror. That means you're not just surviving this world. You're thriving. You're victorious. Not because of your own strength, but because of Jesus. When you choose to live set apart, God fights for you. He vindicates you. He establishes you. Don't shrink back to fit in. Stand tall and stand out for Christ.

Prayer:

Lord, help me to live set apart for You, even when it's uncomfortable or unpopular. Remind me that I am more than a conqueror and that Your love for me never changes. Give me boldness to stand out for You in Jesus name.

Declarations:

- I speak boldness: I will live set apart for God, even if it means standing alone.

- I declare that I am more than a conqueror through Christ, and nothing can separate me from His love.

- I speak this commitment: I will not compromise to fit in; I will stand out for Jesus.

Action Step:

Choose one way to be different for Jesus today. It could be in your words, your choices, or your actions. Be intentional about living set apart.

Journal Space:

DAY 21
The Real Enemy Is Not People

Memory Verse

Your hand-to-hand combat is not with human beings, but with the highest principalities and authorities operating in rebellion under the heavenly realms. For they are a powerful class of demon-gods and evil spirits that hold this dark world in bondage – Ephesians 6:12, TPT.

Bible Reading: *Ephesians 6:10-20*

Devotional:

It's easy to see people as the enemy. That person who gossiped about you. That friend who betrayed you. That teacher who treats you unfairly. But God reminds you that people are not your enemy. Satan is. He's the one stirring up division, hate, and pain. He wants you to focus your anger and energy on people so you miss the real battle. When you realize that the enemy is spiritual, not physical, it changes everything. You stop fighting people and start fighting the forces behind their actions. You forgive instead of retaliating. You pray instead of gossip. You love instead of hate. This doesn't mean you let people hurt you. It means you recognize the bigger picture and fight the real battle with prayer, faith, and love.

Prayer:

Father, I pray that You would open my eyes to see the real enemy. Help me to forgive those who hurt me and to fight the real battle through prayer and love. Give me compassion for people, even when they wrong me in Jesus name.

Declarations:

- I speak clarity: My battle is not against people, but against spiritual forces.

- I declare that I will fight with prayer, forgiveness, and love, not with revenge or hate.

- I speak wisdom: I will see past the actions of people and recognize the enemy's schemes.

Action Step:

Think of someone who has hurt you. Instead of seeking revenge or holding a grudge, pray for them today. Ask God to open their eyes and to heal the situation.

Journal Space:

DAY 22
Truth Sets You Free From Lies

Memory Verse

And you will know the truth, and the truth will set you free – John 8:32, NLT.

Bible Reading: *John 8:31-47*

Devotional:

Lies are chains. The lie that you're not good enough. The lie that you'll never change. The lie that God could never forgive you. The lie that everyone else has it together except you. Satan is the father of lies, and he's been whispering deception since the beginning of time. But Jesus is the truth, and the truth breaks every chain. When you replace the enemy's lies with God's truth, freedom comes. You're not defined by your past. You're not stuck in your sin. You're not worthless. You are loved, redeemed, chosen, and empowered by the truth of God's Word. Stop believing the lies. Start declaring the truth. Write it. Speak it. Meditate on it. The truth will set you free, but you have to choose to believe it.

Prayer:

Lord, help me to recognize the lies I've believed and to replace them with Your truth. Set me free from every chain of deception and anchor me in Your Word. Let Your truth transform my life in Jesus name.

Declarations:

- I speak truth over every lie: I am who God says I am.

- I declare that I will not believe the enemy's lies but will stand firm in God's truth.

- I speak freedom: The truth of God's Word is breaking every chain in my life.

Action Step:

Identify one lie you've believed about yourself (I'm not enough, I'm a failure, I'm unlovable, etc.). Find a Scripture that speaks truth to that lie and write it down. Declare it over yourself today.

Journal Space:

DAY 23
Self-Control Is A Superpower

Memory Verse

But the fruit of the Spirit is love, joy, peace, forbearance, kindness, goodness, faithfulness, 23 gentleness and self-control. Against such things there is no law – Galatians 5:22-23, NIV.

Bible Reading: *Galatians 5:16-26*

Devotional:

Self-control is listed as a fruit of the Spirit, which means it's not something you manufacture on your own. It's something God grows in you. But you have to cooperate. Self-control is the ability to say no to your impulses and yes to what honours God. It's choosing to stop scrolling when you know you need to sleep. It's walking away from the argument instead of firing back. It's saying no to that second helping when you're already full, not because food is bad, but because you're practicing discipline. Self-control is a superpower in a world that worships instant gratification. It sets you apart and positions you for blessing. The more you practice it, the stronger it becomes. Start small. Choose one area today to exercise self-control, and ask the Holy Spirit to help you.

Prayer:

Father, I pray that You would grow the fruit of self-control in my life. Help me to resist my impulses and to make decisions that honour You. Strengthen me through Your Spirit to live a disciplined life in Jesus name.

Declarations:

- I speak self-control over my life: I will not be ruled by my impulses or emotions.

- I declare that the Holy Spirit is strengthening me to make wise, disciplined choices.

- I speak this truth: Self-control is not weakness; it's strength, and it positions me for blessing.

Action Step:

Practice self-control in one area today. It could be your words, your eating, your screen time, or your reactions. Be intentional and ask God to help you.

Journal Space:

DAY 24
Keep Going, Don't Give Up

Memory Verse

And don't allow yourselves to be weary or disheartened in planting good seeds, for the season of reaping the wonderful harvest you've planted is coming! – Galatians 6:9, TPT.

Bible Reading: *Galatians 6:1-10*

Devotional:

You're tired. You've been trying to do the right thing, and it feels like no one notices or cares. You've been standing strong, and it seems like everyone else is getting ahead while you're stuck. You're tempted to quit. To give up. To stop trying. But God says, "Don't become weary." Keep going. Keep doing good. Keep standing firm. Because at the proper time, you will reap a harvest. Not maybe. Not if you're lucky. You will. But only if you don't give up. The world celebrates instant results, but God's promises are for those who endure. Your faithfulness today is planting seeds for tomorrow's harvest. Don't quit before the breakthrough comes. Keep going.

Prayer:

Lord, help me to keep going when I'm weary and discouraged. Remind me that You see every effort I make and that my labour is not in vain. Strengthen me to persevere until I see the harvest in Jesus name.

Declarations:

- I speak endurance over my life: I will not quit, even when it's hard.

- I declare that my faithfulness today is creating a harvest for tomorrow.

- I speak this truth: God sees my efforts, and He will honour my perseverance.

Action Step:

Identify one area where you're tempted to give up (a relationship, a goal, your faith walk, etc.). Commit to continuing for one more week and ask God for renewed strength.

Journal Space:

DAY 25
Live In The Freedom Christ Gave You

Memory Verse

So if the Son sets you free, you are free through and through – John 8:36, MSG.

Bible Reading: *John 8:31-36; Galatians 5:1*

Devotional:

Jesus didn't set you free from sin so you could go back to it. He broke the chains so you could walk in freedom. But freedom requires vigilance. The enemy wants you to believe you're still bound, even though you're not. He wants you to go back to the same habits, the same lies, the same sin. Don't fall for it. You are free. Free from guilt. Free from shame. Free from the power of sin. That doesn't mean you'll never mess up, but it means sin no longer has authority over you. You have a choice. Choose freedom. Break the unhealthy habit. Walk away from the toxic relationship. Stop going back to what Jesus already freed you from. Live like the free person you are.

Prayer:

Father, I pray that You would help me to walk in the freedom You've given me. Break every chain that tries to pull me back into bondage. Give me strength to live as the free person I am in Christ, in Jesus name.

Declarations:

- I speak freedom over my life: I am free from sin's power because of Jesus.

- I declare that I will not go back to what God has freed me from.

- I speak this truth: I am walking in the freedom Christ gave me, and I will not be enslaved again.

Action Step:

Identify one unhealthy habit or pattern you keep going back to. Pray about it, then create a plan to break it. Share your plan with someone who will hold you accountable.

Journal Space:

DAY 26
God Can Use You Right Now

Memory Verse

And don't be intimidated by those who are older than you; simply be the example they need to see by being faithful and true in all that you do. Speak the truth and live a life of purity and authentic love as you remain strong in your faith – 1 Timothy 4:12, TPT.

Bible Reading: *1 Timothy 4:11-16*

Devotional:

You might think you're too young to make a real difference. That you need to wait until you're older, more experienced, or more qualified. But God doesn't see it that way. He's been using young people to change the world since the beginning of time. David was a teenager when he defeated Goliath. Mary was likely a teenager when she gave birth to Jesus. Timothy was young when Paul mentored him to lead the church. God doesn't need you to be perfect or polished. He needs you to be willing. Your age is not a disqualification. It's an opportunity. Use your gifts, your passion, and your faith to make an impact now. Don't wait. God can use you right where you are.

Prayer:

Lord, help me to believe that You can use me right now, just as I am. Remove any insecurity or doubt about my age or abilities. Use me to make a difference for Your kingdom today in Jesus name.

Declarations:

- I speak boldness: I will not let my age stop me from serving God.

- I declare that God can use me right now, just as I am.

- I speak this truth: I will set an example in my words, my actions, and my faith.

Action Step:

Use one of your gifts or talents today for God's glory. Serve someone. Encourage someone. Share your faith. Don't wait for "someday." Do it now.

Journal Space:

DAY 27

Joy Is Your Strength, Not Your Circumstance

Memory Verse

Don't be dejected and sad, for the joy of the Lord is your strength! – Nehemiah 8:10, NLT.

Bible Reading: *Nehemiah 8:9-12*

Devotional:

Happiness depends on what's happening. Joy depends on who God is. Happiness is temporary. Joy is eternal. You can have joy even in the middle of pain, struggle, and disappointment because joy isn't rooted in your circumstances. It's rooted in the unchanging character of God. When everything around you is falling apart, joy says, "God is still good. He's still in control. He's still working." The enemy wants to steal your joy because he knows it's your strength. When you lose your joy, you lose your fight. But when you choose joy, even in the hard times, you tap into a supernatural strength that keeps you standing. Stop waiting for everything to be perfect before you choose joy. Choose it now, in the mess, and watch how it changes you.

Prayer:

Father, I pray that You would fill me with Your joy, regardless of my circumstances. Help me to find my strength in You and to choose gratitude even when life is hard. Let Your joy overflow from my life in Jesus name.

Declarations:

- I speak joy over my life: My joy is not dependent on my circumstances but on God's faithfulness.

- I declare that I will choose gratitude over complaining and praise over negativity.

- I speak this truth: The joy of the Lord is my strength, and nothing can take it from me.

Action Step:

Today, choose gratitude instead of complaining. Write down three things you're thankful for, no matter how small, and thank God for them.

Journal Space:

....

....

....

....

....

....

DAY 28
Peace In The Storm

Memory Verse

I leave the gift of peace with you—my peace. Not the kind of fragile peace given by the world, but my perfect peace. Don't yield to fear or be troubled in your hearts—instead, be courageous! – John 14:27, TPT.

Bible Reading: *John 14:25-31*

Devotional:

The world gives temporary peace. "Everything will be okay when you graduate." "You'll feel better when you get that relationship." "Peace will come when life calms down." But Jesus gives a different kind of peace. A peace that doesn't depend on your circumstances. A peace that holds you steady in the middle of the storm. When everything around you is chaos, His peace is your anchor. It's not something you earn or work for. It's a gift. But you have to receive it. You receive it by trusting Him, even when you can't see the way. By surrendering your worry and anxiety to Him. By refusing to let fear control you. Today, in the middle of whatever storm you're facing, receive His peace. It's already yours.

Prayer:

Lord, help me to receive Your perfect peace. When anxiety tries to overwhelm me, remind me that You are in control. Guard my heart and mind with Your peace that surpasses all understanding in Jesus name.

Declarations:

- I speak peace over my mind and my heart: I will not be controlled by anxiety or fear.

- I declare that Jesus' peace is guarding my heart and mind, no matter what I'm facing.

- I speak this truth: I will trust God and refuse to let my heart be troubled.

Action Step:

Take five minutes today in complete silence with God. No phone. No distractions. Just sit, breathe, and invite His peace to fill you.

Journal Space:

DAY 29
Your Life Is A Testimony

Memory Verse

Don't let anyone think less of you because you are young. Be an example to all believers in what you say, in the way you live, in your love, your faith, and your purity – 1 Timothy 4:12, NLT.

Bible Reading: *1 Timothy 4:11-16*

Devotional:

Whether you realize it or not, people are watching you. They're watching how you respond when things don't go your way. How you treat others when no one's looking. How you live out your faith in real life, not just on Sundays. Your life is a testimony, and it speaks louder than your words ever will. You don't have to be perfect, but you do have to be intentional. Be intentional about how you speak. How you act. How you love. How you show your faith. People need to see that Jesus is real, and they'll see it in you if you let Him shine through your life. Don't underestimate the impact of your example. Live in a way that makes people ask, "What's different about you?"

Prayer:

Father, I pray that my life would be a living testimony of Your love and grace. Help me to be intentional in everything I do so that others can see You in me. Use my life to point people to Jesus, in Jesus name.

Declarations:

- I speak boldness: My life will be a testimony of God's goodness and grace.

- I declare that I will live intentionally, setting an example in all I do.

- I speak this truth: People are watching, and I will point them to Jesus through my life.

Action Step:

Be intentional today to live as an example. In your words, your actions, and your attitude, let people see Jesus in you.

Journal Space:

DAY 30
Stand Firm, No Matter What

Memory Verse

Keep your eyes open, hold tight to your convictions, give it all you've got, be resolute, and love without stopping – 1 Corinthians 16:13, MSG.

Bible Reading: *1 Corinthians 16:13-24*

Devotional:

The world will shake. Culture will shift. Trends will change. But your foundation is Jesus, and He never changes. Standing firm doesn't mean you'll never struggle or doubt. It means that no matter what comes, you refuse to abandon your faith. You refuse to compromise. You refuse to walk away. Standing firm requires courage. It requires strength. And it requires constant vigilance because the enemy is always looking for cracks in your armour. But when you stand firm in faith, you become unshakable. You become a force that the enemy can't move. This week, you've been equipped with truth, with encouragement, and with God's Word. Now it's time to stand firm and put it all into practice.

Prayer:

Lord, help me to stand firm in my faith, no matter what challenges come my way. Give me the courage to hold tight to my convictions and to never compromise. Be my unshakable foundation in Jesus name.

Declarations:

- I speak firmness over my faith: I will not be moved by culture, pressure, or doubt.
- I declare that my foundation is Jesus, and He is unshakable.
- I speak this truth: I will stand firm in my faith, no matter what comes my way.

Action Step:

Write down one specific way you will stand firm this week. It could be in a relationship, a decision, or a temptation. Commit to it and ask God to give you strength.

Journal Space:

....

....

....

....

....

....

DAY 31
Victory Belongs To You

Memory Verse

No, despite all these things, overwhelming victory is ours through Christ, who loved us – Romans 8:37, NLT.

Bible Reading: *Romans 8:31-39*

Devotional:

You made it. Thirty-one days of standing strong, fighting battles, and growing in your faith. But this isn't the end. This is just the beginning. The world is still broken. The enemy is still fighting. But here's the truth that anchors everything: You are more than a conqueror. Not because of your strength, but because of Jesus. Nothing can separate you from His love. Not failure. Not sin. Not fear. Not doubt. Nothing. The enemy doesn't have the last word. Jesus does. And His word is victory. So as you step into the rest of your life, remember: You're not fighting for victory. You're fighting from victory. Jesus already won. Now, live like it. Stand strong. Keep fighting. And never forget whose you are.

Prayer:

Father, I pray that You would remind me daily that I am victorious through Christ. Thank You for carrying me through this month and for every victory You've given me. Help me to continue standing strong and living in the victory Jesus has already won in Jesus name.

Declarations:

- I speak victory over my life: I am more than a conqueror through Christ.

- I declare that nothing can separate me from God's love, and I will walk in that truth daily.

- I speak this boldly: The enemy does not have the final say. Jesus does, and He has already won.

Action Step:

Celebrate one victory God has given you this month. Write it down. Thank Him for it. Then, commit to continuing this journey of faith with the same intensity.

Journal Space:

CLOSING THOUGHTS

You did it. Thirty-one days of intentionally pursuing God, standing firm in your faith, and equipping yourself for the battles ahead. That's no small thing. In a world where most people can't stay focused for 31 seconds, you stayed committed for 31 days. Be proud of that. More importantly, recognize that God is proud of you.

But here's the thing: This isn't the finish line. It's the starting line.

The habits you've built over the past month, spending time in God's Word, praying daily, declaring truth, taking action, these aren't just for a 31-day challenge. These are the rhythms that will sustain you for a lifetime. The enemy wants you to think that now that you've finished this devotional, you can go back to autopilot. Don't fall for it. What you've started here is a foundation. Now it's time to build on it.

You're going to face days when you don't feel like praying. Days when reading your Bible feels like a chore. Days when standing firm feels impossible. That's normal. Faith isn't about feelings. It's about commitment. It's about showing up even when you don't feel like it. It's about choosing God's way even when it costs you.

Remember the truths you've learned:

- You are chosen, not forgotten.
- Your identity is in Christ, not in what others think of you.
- You are more than a conqueror through Jesus.
- Victory is already yours because Jesus already won.

The world is still broken. The enemy is still fighting. But you are no longer the same person you were 31 days ago. You've been equipped. You've been strengthened. You've been transformed. Now it's time to walk it out.

Don't just be a hearer of the Word. Be a doer. Live what you've learned. Stand firm in what you've declared. And when you fall, because it's possible, get back up. God's grace is new every morning, and His mercies never fail.

Keep standing strong. Keep fighting the good fight. Keep fixing your eyes on Jesus. And never, ever forget: You're not alone in this battle. God is with you, and He's already won the war.

The best is yet to come. Now go live like the victorious, chosen, set-apart teenager of God that you are.

ABOUT THE AUTHOR

Pastor Adekiitan Adetoyese-Oyedun, affectionately known as 'Kiitan, is an Ordained Pastor of The Redeemed Christian Church of God (RCCG) and currently worships at Rhema Chapel Edmonton, where she serves with deep compassion and spiritual insight. Her ministry is marked by a powerful commitment to intercessory prayer, particularly for women, marriages, and families. As a dedicated prayer champion, she stands in the gap for those navigating the complexities of family life and marital relationships, believing wholeheartedly in the transformative power of prayer.

'Kiitan is also a seasoned leader in food safety and quality management with several years of expertise in food safety, quality assurance, BRCGS, HACCP, SQF, and GFSI within the food industry. She holds a Bachelor of Technology in Food Science and Technology and a Master of Science in Food Safety and Toxicology from the prestigious University of Hong Kong. Known for her meticulous approach and commitment to excellence, she has dedicated her career to ensuring the highest standards in food safety and customer satisfaction.

Together with her husband, Pastor 'Toye Oyedun, Kiitan is co-owner of O.E. Motors Inc. and co-founder of Crescite Professional Services Inc. and Crescite General Holdings Corporation. Their entrepreneurial journey demonstrates that professional success and spiritual devotion can beautifully coexist. As marital coaches and counsellors, they help couples understand personality differences and navigate the beautiful complexities of marriage. She actively participates in mentoring singles toward healthy, God-honouring relationships and champions biblical values in homes worldwide. Her ministry extends into the community through volunteering and her active involvement in Club DJ, a midweek church program that guides and nurtures children who have chosen to follow Christ.

'Kiitan is the host of "Read A Book A Month with Kiitan" podcast, where she encourages spiritual and personal growth through the transformative power of reading. A devoted wife and proud mother of wonderful children whom she calls her "Nations," she seamlessly blends professional excellence with her commitment to family and faith.

When she's not ministering, championing food safety, or making a difference in her community, 'Kiitan finds joy in reading, exploring her culinary creativity in the kitchen, and embarking on exciting adventures with her loving husband. She is more than a professional; she's a force for quality, a beacon of spiritual leadership, and a living example of grace in action.

Contact: authors@crescitebooks.com

www.ingramcontent.com/pod-product-compliance
Lightning Source LLC
Chambersburg PA
CBHW051241030726
47595CB00003B/1019